DEVOTIONS
and
PRAYERS
of
JOHN WESLEY

Compiled and Edited By
DONALD E. DEMARAY

D0963167

BAKER BOOK HOUSE
Grand Rapids, Michigan

Library of Congress Catalog Card
Number: 57-12189

Paperback edition issued
September 1977

ISBN: 0-8010-9597-2

PHOTOLITHOPRINTED BY CUSHING - MALLOY, INC.
ANN ARBOR, MICHIGAN, UNITED STATES OF AMERICA
1977

PREFACE

"Pray without ceasing," John Wesley wrote on the flyleaf of a private diary. Even a quick examination of his **Journal** will reveal that he lived constantly in an attitude of prayer, for he refers to prayer and praying literally dozens of times. In his youth he resolved "to dedicate an hour each morning and evening . . . to prayer," a vow which he kept faithfully throughout his long and very busy life.

Wesley's personal, moment - by - moment experience of God is everywhere evident in his prayers and devotions. This accounts for his wealth of spiritual insight and it is also the source of that personal quality or warmth he is able to capture in his written work. This same rich content of religious experience is evident in his hymns (most of which are translations), his sermons, letters and journal entries. In fact, excellent devotional material may be found almost anywhere in his works. In the Wesleyan literature, the spirit of devotion to God is prominent if not dominant.

The design of this volume follows that of the earlier publication by the Baker Book House, **Devotions and Prayers of Martin Luther.** The aim of both books is to offer the public helpful devotional material arranged to stimulate leisurely meditation. No more than five minutes is required for reading a devotion and the accompanying prayer. There are fifty-two devotions, one for each week of the year. Reading a given devotion and the adjoining prayer over and again through the course of a week will yield rich rewards, such as increased understanding of a segment of divine truth, or progress in the art of meditation, an art we need desperately to develop in this busy age.

This little book can be carried conveniently in pocket or purse where it is readily available for reading on the bus or in the car while going to or from work. In the home it can be left on the bed stand to be read just before retiring, or better still it can be put on the breakfast table to be read before beginning the day's work.

To Mr. Herman Baker of the Baker Book House, I wish to express thanks for suggesting this volume. To Mr. Cornelius Zylstra, Editor for Baker Book House, I am grateful for guidance and encouragement.

Where necessary these devotions and prayers have been adapted to the language pattern of the twentieth century in order to retain Wesley's intent and meaning for our own day.

Donald E. Demaray

The New Birth

1

Jesus answered and said unto him, Verily, verily, I say unto thee, Except a man be born again, he cannot see the kingdom of God. — John 3:3

BEFORE a child is born into the world, he has eyes but sees not; he has ears but does not hear. As soon as he is born, he begins to see the light; his ears are then opened, and he hears; and all the other organs of sense begin to be exercised upon their proper objects. How exactly does the parallel hold! While a man is in a mere natural state, before he is born of God, he has, in a spiritual sense, eyes and sees not; he has ears but hears not. His other spiritual senses are locked up; he is in the same condition as if he had them not.

But as soon as he is born of God, there is a total change. The "eyes of his understanding are opened"; he sees the light of the glory of God. His ears being opened, he is now capable of hearing the inward voice of God, saying, "Be of good cheer; thy sins are forgiven thee."

Prayer

O LORD, seeing there is in Christ Jesus an infinite fullness of all that we can want or wish, O that we may all receive of his fullness, grace upon grace; grace to pardon our sins and subdue our iniquities; to justify our persons and to sanctify our souls. O make us partakers of the inheritance of thy saints. Amen.

Alive to God

Likewise reckon ye also yourselves to be dead indeed unto sin, but alive unto God through Jesus Christ our Lord.—*Romans 6:11*

THE person who feels in his heart the mighty working of the Spirit of God is conscious of a "peace which passeth all understanding." He feels "the love of God shed abroad in his heart by the Holy Ghost, which is given unto him"; and all his spiritual senses are then exercised to discern spiritual good and evil. By the use of these, he is daily increasing in the knowledge of God. And now he may be properly said to live: God having quickened him by His Spirit, he is alive to God through Jesus Christ. He lives a life which the world knows not of, a "life which is hid with Christ in God." God is continually breathing, as it were, upon the soul; and his soul is breathing unto God. Grace is descending into his heart, and prayer and praise ascending to heaven: and by this intercourse between God and man, this fellowship with the Father and the Son, as by a kind of spiritual respiration, the life of God in the soul is sustained; and the child of God grows up, till he comes to the "full measure of the stature of Christ."

Prayer

O GLORIOUS Jesus, in whom we live and without whom we die; quicken our hearts with thy holy love, that we may no longer esteem the vanities of the world, but place our affections entirely on thee, who didst die for our sins and rise again for our justification. Amen.

God's Gifts

Every good gift and every perfect gift is from above, and cometh down from the Father of lights, with whom is no variableness, neither shadow of turning.—*James 1:17*

GOD has intrusted us with various gifts. Such is bodily strength; such are health, a pleasing person, an agreeable manner of speech; such are learning and knowledge in their various degrees, with all the other advantages of education. Such is the influence which we have over others, whether by their love and esteem of us, or by power — power to do the good or hurt, to help or hinder them in the circumstances of life. Add to these that invaluable gift of time, with which God intrusts us from moment to moment. Add, lastly, that on which all the rest depends, and without which they would all be curses, not blessings: namely, the grace of God, the power of His Holy Spirit, which alone worketh in us all that is acceptable in his sight.

Furthermore, eternal things only are our own; with all the temporal gifts we are barely intrusted by another — the Disposer and Lord of all. And he intrusts us with them on this express condition, that we use them only as our Master's goods, and according to the particular directions which he has given us in his Word.

Prayer

ETERNAL and merciful Father, I give thee humble thanks (increase my thankfulness, I beseech thee) for all the blessings, spiritual and temporal, which in the riches of thy mercy, thou hast poured down upon me. Amen.

Our Bodies

4

Know ye not that ye are the temple of God,
and that the Spirit of God dwelleth in you?
— I Corinthians 3:16

GOD has intrusted us with our bodies (those exquisitely wrought machines, so "fearfully and wonderfully made"), with all the powers and members thereof. He has intrusted us with the organs of sense; of sight, hearing, and the rest: but none of these are given us as our own, to be employed according to our own will. None of these are lent us in such a sense as to leave us at liberty to use them as we please for a season. No: we have received them on these very terms, that as long as they abide with us, we should employ them all in that very manner, and no other, which he appoints.

To God we are accountable for the use of our hands and feet, and all the members of our body. These are so many talents which are committed to our trust, until the time appointed by the Father. Until then, we have the use of all these; but as stewards, not as proprietors: to the end, we should "render them, not as instruments of unrighteousness unto sin, but as instruments of righteousness unto God."

Prayer

I HUMBLY and heartily thank thee for all the favors thou hast bestowed on me: for creating me after thine own image, for daily preserving me by thy good providence. I also thank thee for thy temporal blessings; for the preservation of me, for my health, strength, food, raiment, and all the other comforts and necessities of life. Amen.

The Tongue

5

Who have said, With our tongue will we prevail; our lips are our own: who is lord over us? — *Psalm 12:4*

GOD has given us that most excellent talent of speech. "Thou hast given me a tongue," says the ancient writer, "that I may praise thee therewith." For this purpose was it given to all the children of men, to be employed in glorifying God. Nothing, therefore, is more ungrateful or more absurd than to think or say, "Our tongues are our own." That cannot be, unless we have created ourselves, and so are independent of the Most High. Nay, but "It is he that hath made us, and not we ourselves": the manifest consequence is that he is still Lord over us, in this as in all other respects. It follows that there is not a word of our tongue for which we are not accountable to him.

Prayer

O HIDE this self from me, that I
  No more, but Christ in me, may live;
My vile affections crucify,
  Nor let one darling lust survive!
In all things nothing may I see,
  Nothing desire or seek, but thee. Amen.

The Kingdom of Heaven

6

And let the peace of God rule in your hearts . . . . — *Colossians 3:15*

THIS is that kingdom of heaven, or of God, which is within us: even "righteousness, peace, and joy in the Holy Ghost." And what is "righteousness," but the life of God in the soul; the mind which was in Christ Jesus; the image of God stamped upon the heart now renewed after the likeness of him that created it? What is it but the love of God, because he first loved us, and the love of all mankind for his sake?

And what is this "peace," the peace of God, but that calm serenity of soul, that sweet repose in the blood of Jesus, which leaves no doubt of our acceptance in him; which excludes all fear but the loving, filial fear of offending our Father which is in heaven?

This inward kingdom implies also "joy in the Holy Spirit," who seals upon our hearts "the redemption which is in Jesus," the righteousness of Christ given us "for the remission of the sins that are past"; who gives us our inheritance of the crown which the Lord, the righteous Judge, will give at that day.

Prayer

TAKE my poor heart, and let it be
    Forever closed to all but thee;
Seal thou my breast, and let me wear
    That pledge of love forever there. Amen.

The Last Judgment

7

And as it is appointed unto men once to die, but after this the judgment. — *Hebrews 9:27*

AT the Last Judgment we are to give an account of all our works, from the cradle to the grave. Also of all our words, our desires and tempers, all the thoughts and intents of our hearts; of all the use we have made of our various talents, whether of mind, body or fortune — all this we must give account of. In an earthly court it may be possible for some who are guilty to escape for lack of evidence; but in the Heavenly Court there is no lack of evidence. All men with whom you planned the most secret sins now appear before your face. So does your own conscience, a thousand witnesses in one; now no more capable of being either blinded or silenced, but constrained to know and to speak the naked truth. And is conscience as a thousand witnesses? — yea; but God is as a thousand consciences!

Prayer

TEACH us, O God, to use this world without abusing it; and to receive the things needful for the body, without losing our part in thy love, which is better than life itself. Amen.

The Poor In Spirit

8

Blessed are the poor in spirit: for theirs is the kingdom of heaven. — *Matthew 5:3*

WHOSOEVER thou art to whom God hath given to be "poor in spirit," to feel thyself lost, thou hast a right to the kingdom of heaven through the gracious promise of Him who cannot lie. It is purchased for thee by the blood of the Lamb. It is very nigh: thou art on the brink of heaven! Another step, and thou enterest into the kingdom of righteousness, and peace and joy! Art thou all sin? "Behold the Lamb of God, who taketh away the sin of the world"! All unholy? See thy "advocate with the Father, Jesus Christ the righteous"! Art thou unable to atone for the least of thy sins? "He is the propitiation for [all thy] sins." Now believe on the Lord Jesus Christ, and all thy sins are blotted out! Art thou totally unclean in soul and body? Here is the "fountain for sin and uncleanness"! Arise, and wash away thy sins! Stagger no more at the promise through unbelief! Give glory to God! Dare to believe! Now cry out from the ground of thy heart,

Yes, I yield, I yield at last,
Listen to thy speaking blood;
Me, with all my sins, I cast
On my atoning God!

Prayer

FATHER, I have sinned against heaven and am no more worthy to be called thy son. For Jesus Christ's sake, graciously receive me. Accept my imperfect repentance and send thy spirit of adoption into my heart, that I may be owned by thee, call thee Father, and share in the blessings of thy children. Amen.

Self-Examination Concerning Prayer

9   Pray without ceasing. — *I Thessalonians 5:17*

HAVE I prayed with fervor? At going in and out of church? In church? Morning and evening in private? With my friends? Without ceasing? Have I, wherever I was, gone to church morning and evening, unless absolutely impossible? and spent from one hour to three in private? Have I sincerely meant every word of my prayers? Have I prayed with humility, admitting my inability to pray? Have I concluded my prayers in the Savior's name, recognizing that he intercedes for me at the right hand of God?

Have I during the day prayed for humility, faith, hope, love? Do I love my fellow man, do I deny self and am I truly thankful? Have I offered all I do to my Redeemer, begged his assistance in even the small acts, commended my soul to his keeping? Have I done all this carefully (not in haste), seriously (not allowing any interruptions), and as fervently as I could?

Prayer

GIVE me thy strength; give me thy love; and be the motive of all the use I make of my understanding, my affections, my senses, my health, my time, and whatever other talents I have received from thee. Thus only can I fulfill my duty and thy command of loving thee with all my heart, and mind, and soul and strength. Amen.

Give to the Winds Thy Fears

10

Though an host should encamp against me,
my heart shall not fear . . . — Psalm 27:3

GIVE to the winds thy fears;
  Hope, and be undismayed;
God hears thy sighs and counts thy tears,
  God shall lift up thy head;
Thro' waves and clouds and storms,
  He gently clears thy way;
Wait thou his time, so shall this night
  Soon end in joyous day.

Still heavy is thy heart?
  Still sink thy spirits down?
Cast off thy weight, let fear depart,
  And ev'ry care be gone.
What tho' thou rulest not,
  Yet heav'n and earth and hell
Proclaim, "God sitteth on the throne,
  And ruleth all things well."

Commit thou all thy griefs
  And ways into his hands,
To his sure trust and tender care
  Who earth and heav'n commands;
Who points the clouds their course,
  Whom winds and seas obey;
He shall direct thy wan'dring feet,
  He shall prepare thy way.

Prayer

DELIVER us, we beseech thee, from worldly cares and foolish desires, from vain hopes and causeless fears, and so dispose our hearts that death itself may not be dreadful to us. May our hearts be so firmly established in grace that nothing may affright us or shake our constancy. Amen.

Love Hopes the Best

11 Beareth all things, believeth all things, hopeth all things, endureth all things. — *I Corinthians 13:7*

LOVE "hopeth all things." Is any evil related of any man? Love hopes that the relation is not true, that the thing related was never done. Is it certain it was? But perhaps it was not done with such circumstances as are related; so that allowing the fact, there is room to hope it was not so ill as it is represented. Was the action apparently, undeniably evil? Love hopes the intention was not so. Is it clear the design was evil too? Yet might it not spring, not from the settled temper of the heart, but from a start of passion, or from some vehement temptation, which hurried the man beyond himself? And even when it cannot be doubted but all the actions, designs and tempers are equally evil, still love hopes that God will at last make bare his arm and get himself the victory; and that there shall be "joy in heaven over [this] one sinner that repenteth, more than over ninety and nine just persons that need no repentance."

Prayer

LET thy unwearied and tender love to me make my love unwearied and tender to my neighbor, zealous to pray for and to procure and promote his health and safety, ease and happiness. Make me peaceable and reconcilable, easy to forgive, and glad to return good for evil. Amen.

God's Grace

12

By grace are ye saved through faith. —
Ephesians 2:8

ALL the blessings which God hath bestowed upon man are of his mere grace,
bounty or favor; his free, undeserved favor;
man having no claim to the least of his
mercies. It was free grace that "formed
man of the dust of the ground" and stamped on his soul the image of God. The same
free grace continues to us, at this day, life
and breath, and all things. For there is
nothing we are or have or do which can
deserve the least thing at God's hand. Moreover, whatever righteousness may be found
in man, this is also the gift of God.

If then sinful men find favor with God, it
is "grace upon grace"! If God chooses to
pour fresh blessings upon us, even the
greatest of blessings, salvation, what can
we say but, "Thanks be unto God for his
unspeakable gift!"? "By grace, then, are
ye saved, through faith." Grace is the
source, faith the condition of salvation.

Prayer

SEND thy Holy Spirit to be the guide of all my ways and the sanctifier of my soul and body. Save, defend and build me up in thy fear and love. Give unto me the light of thy countenance, peace from heaven, and the salvation of my soul in the day of the Lord Jesus. Amen.

The Love of Neighbor

13

And the second [commandment] is like unto it, Thou shalt love thy neighbor as thyself. — Matthew 22:39

OUR Lord said, "Thou shalt love thy neighbor as thyself." If any man ask, Who is my neighbor? we reply, every man in the world. Nor may we in any wise except our enemies, or the enemies of God and their own souls. But every Christian loves these also as himself, even "as Christ loved us." He that would more fully understand what manner of love this is, may consider St. Paul's description of it. It is "longsuffering and kind." It "envieth not." It is not rash or hasty in judging. It "is not puffed up," but makes him humble and the servant of all. Love "doth not behave itself unseemly," but becomes "all things to all men." She "seeketh not her own," but only the good of others, that they may be saved. Love is not provoked. It "thinketh no evil." It "rejoiceth not in iniquity, but rejoiceth in the truth." It "beareth all things, believeth all things, hopeth all things, endureth all things."

Prayer

MAY there ever abide in us such a strong and powerful sense of thy mighty love toward us in Christ Jesus as may constrain us freely and willingly to please thee in the constant exercise of righteousness and mercy, temperance and charity, meekness and patience, truth and fidelity, together with such a humble, content, and peaceable spirit as may adorn the religion of our Lord and Master. Amen.

Peace

14
Therefore being justified by faith, we have peace with God through our Lord Jesus Christ. — *Romans 5:1*

P EACE is a fruit of living faith. This indeed our Lord himself, the night before his death, solemnly bequeathed to all his followers: "Peace I leave with you" (you who "believe in God," and "believe also in me") "my peace I give unto you. Not as the world giveth give I unto you. Let not your heart be troubled, neither let it be afraid." And again, "These things have I spoken unto you that in me ye might have peace." This is that "peace of God which passeth all understanding," that serenity of soul which it has not entered into the heart of a natural man to conceive, and which it is not possible for even the spiritual man to utter. And it is a peace which all the powers of earth and hell are unable to take from him. Waves and storms beat upon it, but they shake it not; for it is founded upon a rock. It keeps the hearts and minds of the children of God at all times and in all places. Whether they are in ease or in pain, in sickness or health, in abundance or want, they are happy in God.

Prayer

THOU hast declared thou wilt accept the sacrifice of thanksgiving in return for all thy goodness. Forever, therefore, will I bless thee, will I adore thy power and magnify thy goodness. My tongue shall sing of thy righteousness and be telling of thy salvation from day to day. I will give thanks unto thee forever and ever; I will praise my God while I have my being. Amen.

Homo Unius Libri

15

And that from a child thou hast known the holy scriptures, which are able to make thee wise unto salvation through faith which is in Christ Jesus. — II Timothy 3:15

I WANT to know one thing, the way to heaven: how to land safely on that happy shore. God himself has condescended to teach the way; for this very purpose he came from heaven. He has written it down in a book! O give me that book! At any price, give me the book of God! I have it: here is knowledge enough for me. Let me be **homo unius libri,** a man of one book. Here then I am, far from the busy ways of men. I sit down alone: only God is here. In his presence I open, I read his book to find the way to heaven. Is there a doubt concerning the meaning of what I read? I lift up my heart to the Father of lights — Lord, is it not thy word, "If any man lack wisdom, let him ask of God"? Thou "givest liberally, and upbraidest not." Thou hast said, "If any be willing to do thy will, he shall know." I am willing to do; let me know thy will.

Prayer

WE offer up our souls and bodies to thee, to be governed, not by our own will, but thine. Let it ever be the joy of our hearts to be under the conduct of thine unerring wisdom, to follow thy counsels and to be ruled in all things by thy holy will. And let us never distrust thy abundant kindness and tender care over us. Amen.

Born of the Spirit

16

That which is born of the flesh is flesh; and that which is born of the Spirit is spirit. — John 3:6

WHAT does it mean to be born of the Spirit? It is that great change which God works in the soul when he brings it into life; when he raises it from the death of sin to the life of righteousness. It is the change wrought in the whole soul by the almighty Spirit of God, when it is "created anew in Christ Jesus," when it is "renewed after the image of God, in righteousness and true holiness"; when the love of the world is changed into the love of God; pride into humility; passion into meekness; hatred, envy, malice, into a sincere, tender, disinterested love for all mankind. In a word, it is that change whereby the earthly, sensual, devilish mind is turned into the "mind which was in Christ Jesus." This is the nature of the new birth: "So is everyone that is born of the Spirit."

Prayer

IS there a thing beneath the sun
  That strives with thee my heart to share?
Ah, tear it thence, and reign alone.
  The Lord of every motion there!
Then shall my heart from earth be free,
  When it hath found repose in thee. Amen.

Happiness

Happy is he that hath the God of Jacob for his help, whose hope is in the Lord his God. — *Psalm 146:5*

As there is but one God in heaven above and in the earth beneath, so there is only one happiness for created spirits, either in heaven or earth. This one God made our heart for himself, and it cannot rest till it resteth in him. It is true that while we are in the vigor of youth and health; while our blood dances in our veins; while the world smiles upon us, and we have all the conveniences, yea, and superfluities of life: we frequently have pleasing dreams and enjoy a kind of happiness. But it cannot continue; it flies away like a shadow: and even while it does, it is not solid or substantial: it does not satisfy the soul. We still pant after something else, something which we have not. Give a man everything that this world can give, yet

> Amidst our plenty something still,
>   To me, to thee, to him is wanting.

That **something** is neither more nor less than the knowledge and love of God, without which no spirit can be happy either in heaven or earth.

Prayer

WE desire, O God, thy good for our lives. Pity our follies; deliver us from our miseries and forgive us our sins. Hear the cry of our hearts and bring us all into the glorious liberty of the sons of God. Amen.

18 O Lord my God, I cried unto thee, and thou hast healed me. — *Psalm 30:2*

FROM John Wesley's **Journal:**

Sunday, May 10, 1741. Being ill, I was obliged to lie down for most of the day. Yet in the evening my weakness was suspended, while I was calling sinners to repentance. But at our love-feast which followed, beside the pain in my back and head, and the fever which still continued, I was seized with such a cough that I could hardly speak. I called on Jesus aloud to "increase my faith," and to "confirm the word of his grace." While I was speaking, my pain vanished, the fever left me, my bodily strength returned and for many weeks I felt neither weakness nor pain. "Unto thee, O Lord, do I give thanks."

Sunday, October 3, 1756. My disorder returned as violent as ever, but I regarded it not while I was performing the service at Snowfields in the morning, or afterward at Spitalfields, until I went to the table to administer the Lord's Supper. A thought then came into my mind: Why do I not ask God for help at the beginning rather than at the end of my illness? I did so, and found immediate relief so that I needed no further medicines.

Prayer

O MOST great and glorious God, who art mighty in thy power and wonderful in thy doings toward the sons of men; accept, I beseech thee, my unfeigned thanks and praise for my creation, preservation, and all the other blessings which in the riches of thy mercy thou hast from time to time poured down upon me. Amen.

The Love of God

19

Jesus said unto him, Thou shalt love the Lord thy God with all thy heart, and with all thy soul, and with all thy mind. — Matthew 22:37

TRUE love of God engrosses the whole heart, takes up all the affections, fills the entire capacity of the soul, and employs the utmost extent of all its facilities. He who thus loves the Lord, continually "rejoiceth in God his Savior." His delight is in the Lord, his Lord and his All, to whom "in every thing he giveth thanks." "All his desire is unto God, and to the remembrance of his name." His heart is ever crying out, "Whom have I in heaven but thee, and there is none upon earth that I desire beside thee." Indeed, what can he desire beside God? Not the world, or the things of the world. For he is "crucified to the world, and the world crucified to him." He is crucified to the desire of the flesh, the desire of the eye, and the pride of life. Yea, he is dead to pride of every kind; for, "love is not puffed up;" but "he that, dwelling in love, dwelleth in God, and God in him," is less than nothing in his own eyes.

Prayer

DELIVER me, O God, from all idolatrous love of any creature. Preserve me from all such blind affection. Be thou a guard to all my desires. And be thou my security, that I may never open my heart to anything but out of love to thee. Amen.

No Limit to Endurance

20

Beareth all things, believeth all things, hopeth all things, endureth all things. — I Corinthians 13:7

LOVE "endureth all things." Love endures not some, not many things only, not most, but absolutely **all things.** Whatever the injustice, the malice, the cruelty of men can inflict, he is able to suffer. He calls nothing intolerable; he never says of anything, "This is not to be borne." No: He cannot only do but suffer all things through Christ which strengtheneth him. And all he suffers does not destroy his love, nor impair it in the least. It is proof against all. It is a flame that burns even in the midst of the great deep. "Many waters cannot quench" his "love, neither can the floods drown it."

Thus in obedience to what Heaven decrees,
Knowledge shall fail, and prophecy shall cease;
But lasting charity's more ample sway —
Nor bound by time, nor subject to decay —
In happy triumph shall forever live,
And endless good diffuse, and endless praise
    receive.

Prayer

EACH moment draw from earth away
 My heart, that lowly waits thy call;
Speak to my inmost soul, and say,
 "I am thy Love, thy God, thy All!"
To feel thy power, to hear thy voice,
 To taste thy love, be all my choice. Amen.

Faith and Works

Ye shall know them by their fruits. —
Matthew 7:16

TRUE faith cannot be manufactured by our own thoughts, for it is solely a work of God in us, without any assistance on our part. As Paul says to the Romans, it is God's gift and grace, obtained by one man, Christ. Therefore, faith is something very powerful, active, restless, effective, which at once renews a person and again regenerates him, and leads him altogether into a new manner and character of life, so that it is impossible not to do good without ceasing.

For just as natural as it is for the tree to produce fruit, so natural is it for faith to produce good works. And just as it is quite unnecessary to command the tree to bear fruit, so there is no command given to the believer, as Paul says, nor is urging necessary for him to do good, for he does it of himself, freely and unconstrained; just as he of himself without command sleeps, eats, drinks, puts on his clothes, hears, speaks, goes and comes.

Whoever has not this faith talks but vainly about faith and works.

Prayer

THOU hast sent thine only Son that whosoever believeth in him should not perish but have everlasting life. O Lord, we believe, help our unbelief. Give us true repentance toward God and faith in our Lord Jesus Christ, and let the love of God be shed abroad in our hearts by the Holy Ghost which is given us. Amen.

Reason and the Holy Spirit

22

IS it not reason, assisted by the Holy Spirit, which enables us to understand what the Holy Scriptures declare? It is by reason that God enables us, in some measure, to comprehend his method of dealing with the children of men; the nature of his various dispensations, of the old and new covenant, of the law and the gospel. It is by this we understand (his Spirit opening and enlightening the eyes of our understanding) what that repentance is; what is that faith whereby we are saved; what is the nature and the condition of justification; what are the immediate, and what the subsequent fruits of it. By reason we learn what is that new birth, without which we cannot enter into the kingdom of heaven; and what that holiness is, without which no man shall see the Lord. By the due use of reason we come to know what are the tempers implied in inward holiness, and what it is to be outwardly holy, holy in all manner of conversation: in other words, what is the mind that was in Christ; and what it is to walk as Christ walked.

Prayer

SEND down, O God of our fathers and Lord of mercy, thy wisdom from thy holy heaven and from the seat of thy greatness, to be in us, and labor with us, and teach us what is acceptable unto thee; that we may know our end, and wisely choose our way, and order our actions to our true felicity. Amen.

God and the Weather

In the day of my trouble I will call upon thee: for thou wilt answer me.—*Psalm* 86:7

FROM John Wesley's **Journal** (1755):

April 24. We rode in less than four hours to Newell Hay. Just as I began to preach the sun broke out and shone exceedingly hot on the side of my head. I found, if I continued, I should not be able to speak long, and lifted up my heart to God. In a minute or two it was covered with clouds, which continued until the service was over. Let any one who please, call this chance: I call it an answer to prayer.

April 25. I preached at Hepstonstall, on the brow of the mountain. The rain began almost as soon as I began to speak. I prayed that if God saw best, it might be stayed until I had delivered his word. It was so, and then began again.

April 26. Preached at seven and four P.M. When I began in a meadow near the house, the wind was so high, I could hardly speak. But the winds too are in God's hands: in a few minutes that inconceivably ceased, and we found the Spirit of God breathing in the midst of us, so that great was our rejoicing in the Lord.

Prayer

My Father, I am thy humble servant, whom thou hast preserved, who lives by thy power this day. I bless and glorify thee for thine almighty providence, and humbly pray thee that this and all my days may be wholly devoted to thy service. Amen.

The "Innermost Circle"

24

But the very hairs of your head are all numbered. — *Matthew 10:30*

A PIOUS writer has observed that there is a threefold circle of divine providence. The "outermost circle" includes all the sons of men: heathens, Mohammedans, Jews and Christians. He causes his sun to rise upon all. He gives them rain and fruitful seasons. He pours ten thousand benefits upon them, and fills their hearts with food and gladness. With an "interior circle" he encompasses the whole visible Christian Church; all that name the name of Christ. He has an additional regard to these, and a nearer attention to their welfare. But the "innermost circle" of his providence encloses only the invisible Church of Christ; all real Christians, wherever dispersed in all corners of the earth; all that worship God (of whatever denomination they are) in spirit and in truth. He keeps them as the apple of an eye: he hides them under the shadow of his wings. And it is to these in particular that our Lord says, "Even the hairs of your head are all numbered."

Prayer

O LORD, the God of our salvation, thou still watchest over us for good; thou daily renewest to us our lives and thy mercies; and thou hast given us the assurance of thy word that if we commit our affairs to thee, if we acknowledge thee in all our ways, thou wilt direct our paths. Amen.

Justification by Faith

But the scripture hath concluded all under sin, that the promise by faith of Jesus Christ might be given to them that believe.
— *Galatians 3:22*

THE foundation must be maintained without wavering, that faith without any works, without any merit, reconciles man to God and makes him good. Paul says: "To Abraham, his faith was reckoned for righteousness"; so also with us. Again: "Being therefore justified by faith, we have peace with God through our Lord Jesus Christ." Again: "For with the heart man believeth unto righteousness; and with the mouth confession is made unto salvation." These, and many more similar passages, we must firmly hold and trust in them immovably, so that to faith alone, without any assistance of works, is attributed the forgiveness of sins and our justification.

Therefore the powerful conclusion follows, there must be something far greater and more precious than all good works, by which a man becomes pious and good, before he does good; just as he must first be in bodily health before he can labor and do hard work. This great and precious something is the noble Word of God, which offers us the grace of God in Christ. He who hears and believes this, thereby becomes good and righteous.

Prayer

O LORD, bow down thy gracious eye and pity the frailties of our imperfect nature. Reach forth thy hand and strengthen us with thy grace, that nothing may divert our advance toward thee. In this dangerous labyrinth of the world and the whole course of our pilgrimage here, let thy heavenly dictates be our map and thy holy life be our guide. Amen.

"I Felt My Heart Strangely Warmed"

26

For God so loved the world, that he gave his only begotten Son, that whosoever believeth in him should not perish, but have everlasting life. — John 3:16

FROM John Wesley's **Journal:** (1738)

Monday, Tuesday and Wednesday, I had continual sorrow and heaviness in my heart.

Wednesday May 24. I think it was about five this morning that I opened my Testament on these words, "There are given unto us exceeding great and precious promises, even that ye should be partakers of the divine nature" (II Peter 1:4). Just as I went out, I opened it again on these words, "Thou art not far from the kingdom of God." In the afternoon I was asked to go to St. Paul's Cathedral. The anthem was, "Out of the deep have I called unto thee, O Lord . . . ."

In the evening I went very unwillingly to a society in Aldersgate Street, where one was reading Luther's preface to the Epistle to the Romans. About a quarter before nine, while he was describing the change which God works in the heart through faith in Christ, I felt my heart strangely warmed. I felt I did trust in Christ alone, for salvation; and an assurance was given me that he had taken away my sins, even mine, and saved me from the law of sin and death.

Prayer

WE humble ourselves, O Lord of heaven
and earth, before thy glorious majesty. We
acknowledge thy eternal power, wisdom,
goodness and truth, and desire to render
unto thee thanks for all the benefits which
thou pourest upon us. But, above all, for
thine inestimable love in the redemption of
us by our Lord Jesus Christ. Amen.

First Temptations

The Lord knoweth how to deliver the godly
out of temptations . . . — *II Peter 2:9*

FROM John Wesley's **Journal** directly after his conversion experience:

I began to pray with all my might for those who had in a more especial manner despitefully used me and persecuted me. I then testified openly to all there what I now first felt in my heart. But it was not long before the enemy suggested, "This cannot be faith; for where is thy joy?" Then was I taught that peace and victory over sin are essential to faith, and that the transports of joy which usually attend the beginning of it, especially in those who have mourned deeply, God sometimes gives, sometimes withholds, according to the counsels of his own will.

After my return home, I was much buffeted with temptations; but cried out and they fled. They returned again and again. I as often lifted up my eyes and he "sent me help from his holy place." Herein I found the difference between my present and my former state; then, I was striving, fighting under the law, and sometimes I was conquered. Now, I was always conqueror.

Prayer

THOU knowest, O Lord, all our temptations. Thou knowest the devices of the enemy and the deceitfulness of our own hearts. We pray thee, good Lord, that thou wilt arm us with the whole armor of God. Uphold us with thy free Spirit and watch over us for good evermore. Amen.

Eternal Life

28

And this is life eternal, that they might know thee the only true God, and Jesus Christ whom thou hast sent. — *John 17:3*

ETERNAL life begins when we first know Christ, when we can testify that, "The life which I now live I live by faith in the Son of God." Then it is that happiness begins; happiness real, solid, substantial. Then it is that heaven is opened in the soul, that the heavenly state commences, while the love of God is shed abroad in the heart, instantly producing love to all mankind.

As our knowledge and our love of him increase, the kingdom of an inward heaven must necessarily increase also. When we are **filled with him;** when "Christ is in us, the hope of glory"; when he has taken the full possession of our heart; when he reigns therein without a rival; when we dwell in Christ and Christ in us, we are one with Christ and Christ with us; then we are completely happy; and then we live "all the life that is hid with Christ." Then, and not till then, we experience that "God is love: and whosoever dwelleth in love, dwelleth in God, and God in him."

Prayer

IN Christ's name we come to beg thy pardon and peace, the increase of thy grace and tokens of thy love; for we are not worthy of the least of thy mercies. But worthy is the Lamb that was slain to take away the sin of the world, for whose sake thou wilt give us all things. Amen.

29

And be not conformed to this world: but be ye transformed by the renewing of your mind, that ye may prove what is that good, and acceptable, and perfect, will of God. — *Romans 12:2*

THIS unspeakable folly of preferring present things to eternal is the disease of every man born into the world. The eye sees distinctly the space that is near it, with the objects which it contains. The eye, however, does not see the beauties of China; they are at too great a distance. For the same reason the mind does not see either the beauties or the terrors of eternity. We are not at all affected by them, because they are so distant from us. On this account it is that they appear to us nothing: just as if they had no existence. Meantime we are wholly taken up with things present, whether in time or space; and things appear less and less, as they are more and more distant from us. And so it must be; such is the constitution of our nature; till nature is changed by almighty grace. But this is no manner of excuse for those who continue in their natural blindness to futurity; because a remedy for it is provided, which is found by all that seek it: yea, it is freely given to all that sincerely ask it.

Prayer

O GOD, whose eternal providence has embarked our souls in the ship of our bodies, prevent us from anchoring in any sea of this world, but help us to steer directly through it to thy glorious kingdom; preserve us from the dangers that on all sides assault us, and keep our affections still fitly disposed to receive thy holy inspirations, that being carried strongly forward by thy Holy Spirit we may happily arrive at last in the haven of eternal salvation, through our Lord Jesus Christ. Amen.

Holiness of Life

30

For God hath not called us unto uncleanness, but unto holiness. — *I Thessalonians 4:7*

THERE can be no point of greater importance to him who knows that it is the Holy Spirit which leads us into all truth and into all holiness, than to consider with what temper of soul we are to entertain his divine presence, so as not either to drive him from us, or to disappoint him of the gracious ends for which his abode with us is designed; which is not the amusement of our understanding, but the conversion and entire sanctification of our hearts and lives.

The title "Holy," applied to the Spirit of God, does not only denote that he is holy in his own nature, but that he makes us so: that he is the great fountain of holiness to his Church; the Spirit from whence flows all the grace and virtue by which the stains of guilt are cleansed, and we are renewed in all holy dispositions, and again bear the image of our Creator. The highest obligation lies upon us all to consider holiness of life with the deepest attention.

Prayer

SEND thy Holy Spirit to be the guide of all my ways and the sanctifier of my soul and body. Save, defend, and build me up in thy fear and love. Give unto me the light of thy countenance, peace from heaven, and the salvation of my soul in the day of the Lord Jesus. Amen.

Jesus, Thy Blood and Righteousness

31

Take heed therefore unto yourselves, and to all the flock, over the which the Holy Ghost hath made you overseers, to feed the church of God, which he hath purchased with his own blood. — *Acts 20:28*

JESUS, thy blood and righteousness
My beauty are, my glorious dress,
Midst flaming worlds, in these arrayed,
With joy shall I lift up my head.

Bold shall I stand in thy great day,
For who aught to my charge shall lay?
Fully absolved thro' these I am,
From sin and fear, from guilt and shame.

Lord, I believe thy precious blood,
Which at the mercy seat of God,
Forever doth for sinners plead,
For me e'en for my soul was shed.

Lord, I believe were sinners more
Than sands upon the ocean shore,
Thou hast for all a ransom paid,
For all a full atonement made.

Prayer

THOU art never weary, O Lord, of doing us good. Let us never be weary of doing thee service. Let us take pleasure in thy service and abound in thy work and in thy love and praise evermore. Fill up all that is wanting, reform whatever is amiss in us, perfect the thing that concerns us, and let the witness of thy pardoning love ever abide in all our hearts. Amen.

What Is Faith?

32

Now faith is the substance of things hoped for, the evidence of things not seen. — *Hebrews 11:1*

FAITH in general is defined by the apostle as a divine evidence or conviction of things not seen. This implies both a supernatural evidence of God, and of the things of God; a kind of spiritual light exhibited to the soul. St. Paul says, "God, who commanded light to shine out of darkness, hath shined in our hearts, to give us the light of the knowledge of the glory of God in the face of Jesus Christ." And elsewhere the same apostle speaks of "the eyes of understanding being opened." By this twofold operation of the Holy Spirit, having the eyes of our soul both **opened** and **enlightened,** we see the things which the natural "eye hath not seen, neither the ear heard." We have a prospect of the invisible things of God; we see the spiritual world, which is all around about us, and yet no more discerned by our natural faculties than if it had no being: and we see the eternal world, piercing through the veil which hangs between time and eternity. Clouds and darkness then rest upon it no more, but we already see the glory which shall be revealed.

Prayer

BEHOLD, O Lord, we believe; perfect by thy vigorous grace our faint endeavors. Bring us where our dark faith shall cease into vision and our hope expire into full enjoyment, where all our affections shall be contracted into love and love shall be extended to all eternity. Amen.

Which Eternity?

33

> For he that soweth to his flesh shall of the flesh reap corruption; but he that soweth to the Spirit shall of the Spirit reap life everlasting. — *Galatians 6:8*

WHAT then is he, how foolish, how mad, in how unutterable a degree of distraction, who, seeming to have the understanding of a man, deliberately prefers temporal things to eternal? Especially when we take this into the consideration (which, indeed, should never be forgotten) that the refusing of a happy eternity implies the choosing of a miserable eternity: for there is not, cannot be, any medium between everlasting joy and everlasting pain. It is a vain thought which some have entertained, that death will put an end to the soul as well as to the body. It will put an end to neither the one nor the other; it will only alter the manner of their existence. But when the body "returns to the dust as it was, the spirit will return to God that gave it." Therefore, at the moment of death, it must be unspeakably happy, or unspeakably miserable: and that misery will never end.

> **Never!** Where sinks the soul at that dread sound?
> Into a gulf how dark, and how profound.

How often would he who had made the wretched choice wish for the death both of his soul and body!

Prayer

SEARCH us, O Lord, and prove us. Look well if there be any wickedness in us, and lead us in the way everlasting. Let thy favor be better to us than life itself, that so in all things we may approve our hearts before thee and feel the sense of thy acceptance of us, giving us a joy which the world cannot give. Amen.

Jesus, Thy Boundless Love to Me

34 For the love of Christ constraineth us. —
II Corinthians 5:14

JESUS, thy boundless love to me
No thought can reach, no tongue declare;
O knit my thankful heart to thee,
And reign without a rival there!
Thine, wholly thine alone I'd live,
Myself to thee entirely give.

O grant that nothing in my soul
May dwell, but thy pure love alone;
O may thy love possess me whole.
My joy, my treasure, and my crown.
All coldness from my heart remove;
May every act, word, thought, be love.

O Love, how gracious is thy way!
All fear before thy presence flies;
Care, anguish, sorrow, melt away,
Where'er thy healing beams arise,
O Jesus, nothing may I see,
Nothing desire or seek, but thee.

In suff'ring be thy love my peace;
In weakness be thy love my pow'r;
And when the storms of life shall cease,
Jesus, in that important hour,
In death as life be thou my guide,
And save me, who for me hast died.

Prayer

TAKE thou the full possession of my heart, raise there thy throne, and command there as thou dost in heaven. Being created by thee, let me live to thee. Being created for thee, let me ever act for thy glory. Being redeemed by thee, let me render unto thee what is thine, and let my spirit ever cleave to thee alone. Amen.

Belief In God

35

But as many as received him, to them gave he power to become the sons of God, even to them that believe on his name. — *John 1:12*

WE cannot serve God unless we **believe** in him. This is the only true foundation of serving him. Furthermore, to believe in God implies trust in him as our strength, for without him we can do nothing. Every moment he endues us with power from on high. As our help, our only help in time of trouble, he surrounds us with songs of deliverance. As our shield, our defender, he lifts us above all our enemies.

To believe or trust in God is our happiness. He is the center around which we adjust our lives. He provides rest for our souls. He is the only one who is able to meet our needs adequately, and he the One wholly sufficient to satisfy the desires of our hearts.

To believe in God implies trust in him as the very purpose of our lives. Belief means to have an eye to him in all things; to use all things only as means of enjoying him; wherever we are or whatever we do, to see him who though invisible is looking on us well pleased, and to put all our burdens at his feet.

Prayer

STILL let thy wisdom be my guide,
Nor take thy flight from me away;
Still with me let thy grace abide,
That I from thee may never stray:
Let thy word richly in me dwell,
Thy peace and love my portion be;
My joy to endure and do thy will,
Till perfect I am found in thee. Amen

Personal Faith

36

FAITH in general is a divine, supernatural evidence or conviction "of things not seen," not discoverable by our bodily senses, as being either past, future or spiritual. Justifying faith implies not only a divine evidence or conviction that "god was in Christ reconciling the world unto himself," but a sure trust and confidence that Christ died for **my** sins, that he loved **me,** and gave himself for **me.** And at whatsoever time a sinner thus believes, be it in early childhood, in the strength of his years, or when he is old and white-haired, God justified that ungodly one: God, for the sake of his Son, pardons and absolves him who up to now had no good thing in him. Whatever good he does from that hour when he first believes in God through Christ, faith does not **find** but **brings.** This is the fruit of faith. First the tree is good, and then the fruit is good also.

Prayer

O GOD, purify my heart that I may entirely love thee and rejoice in being loved of thee; that I may confide in thee, and absolutely resign myself to thee, and be filled with constant devotion toward thee; that I may never sink into a base love of anything here below nor be oppressed with the cares of this life; but assist me to abhor that which is evil and cleave to that which is good. Amen.

"I Thirst, Thou Wounded Lamb of God"

37

For ye know the grace of our Lord Jesus Christ, that, though he was rich, yet for your sakes he became poor, that ye through his poverty might be rich. — II Corinthians 8:9

I THIRST, thou wounded Lamb of God,
To wash me in thy cleansing blood;
To dwell within thy wounds; then pain
Is sweet, and life or death is gain.

Take my poor heart, and let it be
Forever closed to all but thee;
Seal thou my breast, and let me wear
That pledge of love forever there.

How blest are they who still abide
Close sheltered in thy bleeding side,
Who thence their life and strength derive,
And by thee move, and in thee live!

What are our works but sin and death,
Till thou thy quick'ning Spirit breathe?
Thou giv'st the pow'r thy grace to move:
O wondrous grace! O boundless love!

Hence our hearts melt, our eyes o'erflow,
Our words are lost, nor will we know,
Nor will we think of aught beside,
My Lord, my Love, is crucified.

Prayer

O SAVIOR of the world, thou that hast destroyed the power of the devil, that hast overcome death, that sitteth at the right hand of the Father, thou that wilt speedily come down in thy Father's glory to judge all men according to their works; be thou my light and my peace. Destroy the power of the devil in me and make me a new creature. Amen.

Victory Over Sin

38
Likewise reckon ye also yourselves to be dead indeed unto sin, but alive unto God through Jesus Christ our Lord.—*Romans 6:11*

AN immediate and constant fruit of the faith whereby we are born of God, a fruit which can in no wise be separated from it, no, not for an hour, is power over sin — power over outward sin of every kind, over every evil word and work. Wheresoever the blood of Christ is thus applied, it "purgeth the conscience from dead works" and inward sin, for the heart is purified from every unholy desire and temper. This fruit of faith St. Paul describes in the sixth chapter of Romans. "How shall we," says he, "who (by faith) are dead to sin, live any longer therein?" "Our old man is crucified with Christ, that the body of sin might be destroyed, that henceforth we should not serve sin." "Likewise reckon ye yourselves to be dead unto sin, but alive unto God through Jesus Christ our Lord. Let not sin therefore reign (even) in your mortal body," "but yield yourselves unto God as those that are alive from the dead." "For sin shall not have dominion over you. God be thanked that ye were the servants of sin—but being made free"—the plain meaning is, God be thanked that though you were in time past the servants of sin, now "being free from sin, ye are become the servants of righteousness."

Prayer

O LORD, my judge, thou art also my redeemer. I have sinned, but thou, O blessed Jesus, art my advocate. Gracious Lord, spare thy servant whom thou hast redeemed with thy most precious blood. Deliver me from the power of sin and preserve me from the punishment of it. Amen.

On Glorifying God

39

I will praise thee, O Lord my God, with all my heart: and I will glorify thy name for evermore. — *Psalm 86:12*

BRETHREN, "Who is an understanding man and endued with knowledge among you," Let him show the wisdom from above by walking suitably to his character. If he considers himself a steward of the manifold gifts of God, let him see that all his thoughts, and words, and works, be agreeable to the post God has assigned him. It is no small thing to thank God with your heart and by your actions for everything you have received from him. This requires all your wisdom, all your resolution, all your patience, and constancy—far more than ever you had by nature—but not more than you may have by grace. For his grace is sufficient for you, and "all things," you know, "are possible to him that believeth." By faith, then, "put on the Lord Jesus Christ," "put on the whole armor of God" and you will be enabled to glorify him in all your words and works; indeed you will even be able to bring every thought into captivity to the obedience of Christ!

Prayer

ACCEPT, O Lord, my gratitude for all the benefits thou hast given me, for the good things of this life and the hope of eternal happiness. To thy holy name be ascribed the honor and glory. Oh, let the sense of all thy blessings have this effect upon me —to make me daily more diligent in devoting myself, all I am, and all I have to thy glory. Amen.

The Witness of the Spirit

40

The Spirit itself beareth witness with our spirit, that we are the children of God. — Romans 8:16

THE man who has just experienced the New Birth hears his Master say, "Be of good cheer; thy sins are forgiven thee; Go and sin no more." This is the purport of what God speaks to his heart, although perhaps not in these very words. He is now ready to hear whatsoever "He that teacheth man knowledge" is pleased from time to time to reveal to him. He "feels in his heart" (to use the language of our Church) "the mighty working of the Spirit of God": not in a gross, carnal sense, as the men of the world stupidly and willfully misunderstand the expression; though they have been told again and again, we mean thereby neither more nor less than this: he feels, is inwardly sensible of, the graces which the Spirit of God works in his heart. He feels, he is conscious of, a "peace which passeth all understanding." He many times feels such a joy in God as is "unspeakable, and full of glory." He feels "the love of God shed abroad in his heart by the Holy Ghost, which is given unto him"; and all his spiritual senses are then exercised to discern spiritual good and evil. By the use of these, he is daily increasing in the knowledge of God, of Jesus Christ whom he hath sent, and of all the things pertaining to his inward kingdom.

Prayer

We implore thy tender mercies in the forgiveness of all our sins and we desire to devote our whole man, body, soul, and spirit, to thee. As thou dost inspire us with these desires, so accompany them always with thy grace, that we may every day with our whole hearts give ourselves up to thy service. Amen.

Wisdom, Love, Power

41

Blessing, and glory, and wisdom, and thanksgiving, and honor, and power, and might,
be unto our God for ever and ever. Amen.
— *Revelation 7:12*

THINE, Lord, is wisdom, thine alone;
Justice and truth before thee stand:
Yet, nearer to thy sacred throne,
Mercy withholds thy lifted hand.

Each evening shows thy tender love,
Each rising morn thy plenteous grace;
Thy wakened wrath doth slowly move,
Thy willing mercy flies apace.

To thy benign, indulgent care,
Father, this light, this breath, we owe;
And all we have, and all we are,
From thee, great Source of being, flow.

Thrice Holy! thine the kingdom is,
The power omnipotent is thine;
And when created nature dies,
Thy never-ceasing glories shine.

Prayer

O LORD our God, thou art infinitely good, and thou hast showed us what is good. Thou sendest out thy light and thy truth that they may guide us. Thou givest us many opportunities to quicken and further us in thy service. Thou hast called and we have refused. And our iniquities become our ruin. Pardon and deliver us. Amen.

Humility

42

Likewise, ye younger, submit yourselves unto the elder. Yea, all of you be subject one to another, and be clothed with humility: for God resisteth the proud, and giveth grace to the humble. — I Peter 5:5

WE learn from Christ to be "lowly of heart." And this is the true, genuine, Christian humility, which flows from a sense of the love of God, reconciled to us in Christ Jesus. Poverty of spirit, in this meaning of the word, begins where a sense of guilt and of the wrath of God ends; and is a continual sense of our total dependence on him for every good thought, or word or work. With this is joined a loving shame, a tender humiliation before God, even for the sins which we know he has forgiven us, and for the sin which still remains in our hearts. Nevertheless, the conviction we feel of inbred sin is deeper and deeper every day. The more we grow in grace, the more do we see of the desperate wickedness of our heart. The more we advance in the knowledge and love of God through our Lord Jesus Christ (as great a mystery as this may appear to those who know not the power of God unto salvation) the more do we discern of our alienation from God—of the enmity that is in our carnal mind, and the necessity of our being entirely renewed in righteousness and true holiness.

Prayer

My soul before thee prostrate lies;
To thee, her Source, my spirit flies;
My wants I mourn, my chains I see;
O let thy presence set me free.

Jesus, vouchsafe my heart and will
With thy meek lowliness to fill;
No more her power let nature boast,
But in thy will may mine be lost. Amen.

Sanctification

43

Let us go on unto perfection. — *Hebrews 6:1*

FROM the time of our being born again, the gradual work of sanctification takes place. We are enabled "by the Spirit to mortify the deeds of the body," of our evil nature; and as we are more and more dead to sin, we are more and more alive to God. We go on from grace to grace, while we are careful to "abstain from all appearance of evil," and are "zealous of good works," as we have opportunity of doing good to all men; while we walk in all his ordinances blameless, therein worshipping him in spirit and truth; while we take up our cross, and deny ourselves every pleasure that does not lead us to God.

It is thus that we wait for entire sanctification; for a full salvation from all our sins —from pride, self-will, anger, unbelief; or as the apostle expresses it, "go on unto perfection." But what is perfection? The word has various senses: here it means perfect love. It is love excluding sin; love filling the heart, taking up the whole capacity of the soul. It is love "rejoicing evermore, praying without ceasing, in every thing giving thanks."

Prayer

O GOD, fill my soul with so entire a love
of thee that I may love nothing but for thy
sake. Give me grace to study thy knowledge daily, that the more I know thee, the
more I may love thee. Let it be the one
business of my life to glorify thee, by every
word of my tongue and by every work of
my hand. Amen.

Prayer and Hypocrisy

44

Moreover when ye fast, be not, as the hypocrites, of a sad countenance: for they disfigure their faces, that they may appear unto men to fast. Verily I say unto you, They have their reward. — *Matthew 6:16*

"AND when thou prayest," said our Lord, "thou shalt not be as the hypocrites are: for they love to pray standing in the synagogues and in the corners of the streets, that they may be seen of men." "Thou shalt not be as the hypocrites are." Hypocrisy or insincerity is the first thing we are to guard against in prayer. Beware not to speak what you do not mean. Prayer is the lifting up of the heart to God: all words of prayer without this are mere hypocrisy. Whenever therefore thou attemptest to pray, see that it be thy one design to commune with God, to lift up thy heart to him, to pour out thy soul before him; not as the hypocrites, who love or are wont "to pray standing in the synagogues," the exchange or market-places, "and in the corners of the streets," wherever the most people are, "that they may be seen of men." This was the sole design, the motive and end of the prayers which they there repeated. "Verily I say unto you, They have their reward." They are to expect no reward from your Father which is in heaven.

Prayer

WE depend upon thee, especially for the grace of thy Holy Spirit. May we feel it perpetually bearing us up, by the strength of our faith, above the temptations that may at any time assault us. Amen.

Christian Meekness

45

The meek will he guide in judgment: and the meek will he teach his way.—*Psalm 25:9*

CHRISTIAN meekness does not imply being without zeal for God any more than it does ignorance or insensibility. No, it keeps clear of every extreme, whether in excess or defect. It does not destroy, but balances the affections, which the God of nature never designed should be rooted out by grace, but only brought and kept under due regulations. It poises the mind aright. It holds an even scale with regard to anger, sorrow and fear; preserving the mean in every circumstance of life, and not declining either to the right hand or to the left. Meekness, therefore, seems properly to relate to ourselves: but it may be referred either to God or our neighbor. When this due composure of mind has reference to God, it is usually termed resignation; a calm acquiescence in whatsoever is his will concerning us, even though it may not be pleasing to nature; saying continually, "It is the Lord; let him do what seemeth him good." When we consider meekness more strictly with regard to ourselves, we style it patience or contentedness. When it is exerted toward other men, then it is mildness to the good, and gentleness to the evil.

Prayer

LET thy mighty power enable us to do our duty toward thee and toward all men with care, diligence, zeal, and perseverance. Help us to be meek and gentle in our conversation, prudent and discreet in ordering our affairs, observant of thy fatherly providence in everything that befalls us, thankful for thy benefits, patient under thy chastisements, and readily disposed for every good word and work. Amen.

The Christian's Hope

46   For in thee, O Lord, do I hope: thou wilt hear, O Lord my God. — *Psalm 38:15*

ONE Scriptural mark of those who are born of God is hope. Thus St. Peter, speaking to all the children of God who were then scattered abroad, said, "Blessed be the God and Father of our Lord Jesus Christ, which according to his abundant mercy hath begotten us again unto a lively hope" (I Peter 1:3). Note that the hope is a **lively** or **living** one; because there is also a **dead** hope, as well as a dead faith; a hope which is not from God, but from the enemy of God and man; as evidently appears by its fruits; for, as it is the offspring of pride, so it is the parent of every evil word and work; whereas, every man that hath in him this living hope is "holy as he that calleth him is holy": every man that can truly say to his brothers in Christ, "Beloved, now are we the sons of God, and we shall see him as he is," "purifieth himself, even as he is pure."

Prayer

MAY the example of our blessed Savior be always dear to us, that we may cheerfully follow him in every holy temper and delight to do thy will, O God. Let these desires which thou hast given us never die or languish in our hearts, but be kept always alive in their vigor and force by the perpetual inspirations of the Holy Ghost. Amen.

Total Surrender to Christ

47 But seek ye first the kingdom of God, and his righteousness; and all these things shall be added unto you. — *Matthew 6:33*

COME, Savior, Jesus, from above,
Assist me with thy heavenly grace;
Empty my heart of earthly love,
And for thyself prepare the place.

O let thy sacred presence fill,
And set my longing spirit free;
Which pants to have no other will,
But night and day to feast on thee.

While in this region here below,
No other good will I pursue:
I'll bid this world of noise and show,
With all its glittering snares, adieu.

That path with humble speed I'll seek,
In which my Savior's footsteps shine;
Nor will I hear, nor will I speak,
Of any other love but thine.

Henceforth may no profane delight
Divide this consecrated soul;
Possess it thou, who hast the right,
As Lord and Master of the whole.

Nothing on earth do I desire,
But thy pure love within my breast;
This, only this, will I require,
And freely give up all the rest.

Prayer

PARDON, good Lord, all my former sins, and make me every day more zealous and diligent to improve every opportunity of building up my soul in thy faith, love and obedience. Make thyself always present to my mind, and let thy love fill and rule my soul in all those places, companies and employments to which thou callest me. Amen.

A Living Sacrifice

48

I beseech you therefore, brethren, by the
mercies of God, that ye present your bodies
a living sacrifice, holy, acceptable unto
God, which is your reasonable service. —
Romans 12:1

O GOD, what offering shall I give
To thee, the Lord of earth and skies?
My spirit, soul, and flesh receive,
A holy, living sacrifice:
Small as it is, 'tis all my store;
More shouldst thou have, if I had more.

Now then, my God, thou hast my soul:
No longer mine, but thine I am:
Guard thou thine own, possess it whole;
Cheer it with hope, with love inflame.
Thou hast my spirit; there display
Thy glory to the perfect day.

Thou hast my flesh, thy hallowed shrine,
Devoted solely to thy will:
Here let thy light forever shine:
This house still let thy presence fill:
O source of life! live, dwell, and move
In me, till all my life be love.

Prayer

GRANT, O Lord, that I may look for nothing, and resent nothing; that I may go through all the scenes of life, not seeking my own glory, but looking wholly unto thee and acting wholly for thee. Amen.

Be Ready

49

Ye men of Galilee, why stand ye gazing up into heaven? this same Jesus, which is taken up from you into heaven, shall so come in like manner as ye have seen him go into heaven. — *Acts 1:11*

WE know it cannot be long before the Lord will descend with the voice of the archangel and the trumpet of God, when every one of us shall appear before him and give account of his own works. "Wherefore, beloved, seeing ye look for these things," seeing ye know he will come and will not tarry, "be diligent, that ye may be found of him in peace, without spot and blameless." Why should ye not? Why should one of you be found on the left hand, at his appearing? He does not will that any should perish, but that all should come to repentance. Can you doubt this when you remember the Judge of all is likewise the Savior of all? Has he not bought you with his own blood that you may not perish but have everlasting life? Oh make proof of his power! He is not far from any one of us, and he is now come not to condemn but to save the world. He stands in the midst! Sinner, does he not now, even now, knock at the door of your heart? Oh that you may now give yourselves to him who gave himself for you, in humble faith, in holy, active, patient love! So will you rejoice with exceeding joy in his day, when he comes in the clouds of heaven!

Prayer

MOST gracious Lord, who hast so loved the world that thou gavest thyself to redeem it, and humbly tookest upon thee our nature that thou mightest suffer as man for the sins of men for our salvation; do thou fill our souls with a sense of thy wonderful love, that we may live in thy obedience, die in thy favor, and rise again to rejoice with thee forever in thy glory. Amen.

What Is Christian Perfection?

50 But the fruit of the Spirit is love, joy, peace, longsuffering, gentleness, goodness, faith, meekness, temperance: against such there is no law. — *Galatians 5:22-23*

WHAT is the perfection of which man is capable while he dwells in a corruptible body? It is the complying with the kind command, "My son, give me thy heart." It is the "loving the Lord his God with all his heart, and with all his soul, and with all his mind." This is the sum of Christian perfection: it is all the love of God: and as he that loves God loves his brother also, it is inseparably connected with the second, "Thou shalt love thy neighbor as thyself:" thou shalt love every man as thy own soul, as Christ loved us. "On these two commandments hang all the law and the prophets": these contain the whole of Christian perfection.

St. Paul, when writing to the Galatians, places perfection in yet another view. It is the one undivided **fruit of the Spirit,** which he describes thus: "The fruit of the Spirit is love, joy, peace, longsuffering, gentleness, goodness, fidelity" (so the word should be translated here), "meekness, temperance." What a glorious constellation of grace is here! Now suppose all these things to be knit together in one, to be united together in the soul of a believer; this is Christian perfection.

Prayer

O LAMB of God, who both by thy example and precept didst instruct us to be meek and humble; give me grace throughout my whole life in every thought, word, and work to imitate thy meekness and humility. Mortify in me the whole body of pride. Amen.

51

And he answering said, Thou shalt love the Lord thy God with all thy heart, and with all thy soul, and with all thy strength, and with all thy mind; and thy neighbor as thyself. — *Luke 10:27*

REMEMBER that God is love and that the Christian is conformed to his likeness. The Christian is full of love to his neighbor, of universal love; not confined to one sect or party; not restrained to those who agree with him in opinions, in outward modes of worship; or to those who are allied to him by blood or recommended by nearness of place. Neither does he love those only that love him, or are endeared to him by intimacy of acquaintance. But his love resembles that of him whose mercy is over all his works. It soars above all boundaries, embracing neighbors and strangers, friends and enemies: yea, not only the good and gentle, but also the evil and unthankful. For he loves every soul that God has made; every child of man, of whatever place or nation. His love to these, so to all mankind, is in itself generous and disinterested; springing from no view of advantage to himself, from no regard to profit or praise.

Prayer

MAKE us faithful in all our contacts with our neighbors, that we may be ready to do good and bear evil, that we may be just and kind, merciful and meek, peaceable and patient, sober and temperate, humble and self-denying, inoffensive and useful in the world; that so glorifying thee here we may be glorified with thee in thy heavenly kingdom. Amen.

Joy

52

Whom having not seen, ye love; in whom, though now ye see him not, yet believing, ye rejoice with joy unspeakable and full of glory.— *I Peter 1:8*

CHRISTIAN joy is joy in obedience: joy in loving God and keeping his commandments. And yet in keeping them as if we were thereby to fulfill the terms of the covenant of works; as if by any works or righteousness of ours we were to procure pardon and acceptance with God. Not so; we are already pardoned and accepted through the mercy of God in Christ Jesus. Not as if we were by our own obedience to procure life, life from the death of sin; this also we have already through the grace of God. Us "hath he quickened, who were dead in sins"; and now we are "alive to God through Jesus Christ our Lord." But we rejoice in walking according to the covenant of grace, in holy love and happy obedience. We rejoice in knowing that, "being justified through his grace," we have "not received that grace of God in vain"; that God having freely reconciled us to Himself, we run in the strength which he has given us. Indeed, we rejoice, through him who lives in our hearts by faith.

Prayer

LIFT our affections to things above, that we may have perfect contentment in well-doing and patient suffering. Free us from the cares of this world, from all distrust of thy good providence, from repining at anything that befalls us; and enable us in everything to give thanks, believing that all things are ordered wisely and shall work together for good. Amen.